W9-AMO-338

USING MATERIALS

VOLUME 9

John Bassett

GROLIER
EDUCATIONAL

Published 2002 by Grolier Educational
Sherman Turnpike,
Danbury, Connecticut 06816

© 2002 Brown Partworks Limited

FOR BROWN PARTWORKS

Project editor:	Lisa Magloff
Deputy editor:	Jane Scarsbrook
Text editors:	Caroline Beattie, Ben Morgan
Designer:	Joan Curtis
Picture researcher:	Liz Clachan
Illustrations:	Mark Walker
Index:	Kay Ollerenshaw
Design manager:	Lynne Ross
Production manager:	Matt Weyland
Managing editor:	Bridget Giles
Editorial director:	Anne O'Daly
Consultant:	Martyn Wheeler, PhD University of Leicester

Printed and bound in Hong Kong

Set ISBN 0-7172-5608-1
Volume ISBN 0-7172-5617-0

Library of Congress Cataloging-in-Publication Data
Science Activities / Grolier Educational
        p. cm.
        Includes index.
        Contents: v.1. Electricity and magnetism—v.2. Everyday Chemistry—v.3. Force and motion—v.4. Heat and energy—v.5. Inside matter—v.6. Light and color—v.7. Our Environment—v.8. Sound and hearing—v.9. Using materials—v.10. Weather and climate.
ISBN 0-7172-5608-1 (set : alk.paper)—ISBN 0-7172-5609-X (v.1 : alk. paper)—
ISBN 0-7172-5610-3 (v.2 : alk. paper)—ISBN 0-7172-5611-1 (v.3 : alk. paper)—ISBN 0-7172-5612-X (v.4 : alk. paper)—ISBN 0-7172-5613-8 (v.5 : alk. paper)—ISBN 0-7172-5614- 6 (v.6 : alk. paper)—ISBN 0-7172-5615-4 (v.7 : alk. paper)—ISBN 0-7172-5616-2 (v.8 : alk. paper)—ISBN 0-7172-5617-0 (v.9 : alk. paper)—ISBN 0-7172-5618-9 (v.10 : alk. paper)
        1. Science—Study and teaching—Activity programs—Juvenile literature. [1. Science—Experiments. 2. Experiments] I. Grolier Educational (Firm)

LB1585.S335 2002
507.1′2—dc21
                                                        2001040519

ABOUT THIS SET

Science Activities gives children a chance to explore fascinating topics from the world of science using the same methods that professional scientists use to solve problems. This set introduces young scientists to the scientific method by focusing on the importance of planning experiments, conducting them in a rigorous fashion so that a fair test can be carried out, recording all the stages, and organizing and analyzing the data to draw conclusions. Readers will have the chance to conduct exciting and innovative hands-on activities and to learn how to record and analyze their experiments and results in a variety of ways.

Every volume of *Science Activities* contains 10 step-by-step experiments, along with follow-up activities that encourage readers to find out more about the subject. The activities are explained and enhanced with detailed introductory and analysis sections. Colorful photos illustrate each activity, and every book is packed full of pictures and illustrations explaining the details of each topic.

By working fun and educational experiments into the context of the scientific method, anyone using this set can get a feel for how professional scientists go about their work. Most importantly, just have fun!

PICTURE CREDITS

Corbis: 29, Martha Avery 51, Nathan Benn 21, Jose Manuel Sanchis Calvete 12, Philip James Corwin 56, Ric Ergenbright 26, Colin Garratt 5, Angelo Hornak 55, David G. Houser 43, Jacqui Hurst 37, Jeremy Horner 36, Wolfgang Kaehler 11, 22, Bob Krist 43, Karen Huntt Mason 50, Kevin R. Morris 28, Richard T. Nowitz 5, Charles Rotkin 11, 23, Paul Seheult 49, Scott T. Smith front cover, 17, Paul A. Souders 33, 49, Adam Woolfitt 23, Michael S. Yamashita 57; **Science Photo Library:** Andrew McClenaghan 20, George Roos/Peter Arnold Inc. 4, Francoise Sauze 49, Andrew Syred 44; **Sylvia Cordaiy:** 39, Humphrey Evans 6; **Travel Ink:** Martyn Evans 38.

CONTENTS

VOLUME 9
USING MATERIALS

INTRODUCTION

Our ability to make and use a wide variety of materials is one of the things that makes us different from other animals. This book explores the fascinating world of materials and how we use them.

Early humans made use of the natural materials that they found around them, such as the flint and stones used to make these arrowheads.

Everything in the world is made up of matter. Matter is anything that takes up space and has weight. Materials are types of matter that can be made into useful objects, such as glass for windows, fabric for clothing, or concrete for building. Materials do not have to be solid to be useful—they can also be gases or liquids.

All matter is made up of tiny particles called atoms. These particles are so small, they can only be seen by very powerful microscopes called electron microscopes. Only 118 different types of atoms have been discovered by scientists up to now. Of them 92 are natural, and 26 have been artificially created by scientists in a laboratory.

Some materials are made of only one type of atom. We call these materials elements. For example, iron is an element because it contains only iron atoms. However, many materials are not elements but compounds. A compound forms when different types of atoms join together to make particles called molecules. We call this process a chemical reaction. For instance, iron atoms and oxygen atoms from the air can join in a chemical reaction to make the compound iron oxide—better known as rust.

MATERIALS AND PEOPLE

When people first began to use materials thousands of years ago, they did little to change the natural materials they found. Clay, wood, bone, skins, and rock were some of the first materials that people used for building, clothing, cooking, or making weapons for hunting. Over many centuries people found out ways to change these materials by shaping them or cutting them. Later still, they discovered complicated ways to make entirely new materials by using heat or chemical reactions, for example. Today we use thousands of materials that our ancestors had not even dreamed of. We can hardly imagine what life would be like without materials like plastic and steel, but they are actually very new materials.

We use different materials for different purposes because they have different properties. A property is anything about a material that can be described, such as how hard or soft it is, its color or shape, whether it is flexible or stiff, and so on.

It is important to study materials to find out all their properties. Scientists study the atoms and molecules that make up materials to figure out their properties and the best ways of using them.

SAFETY

Some of the experiments in this book involve heat. It is important that you do these experiments carefully to avoid burns or fires. Some experiments use chemicals that can cause irritation to skin and the eyes. Make sure that you are in a place with lots of open windows whenever you are using chemicals. Wear rubber gloves, goggles, or other protective clothing when you are working with chemicals, heat, and sharp tools. Never put anything in your mouth unless the book says that it is okay, even if you think it is safe. Always ask an adult for permission before you carry out any experiment.

The materials in this glass are in two states: solid ice and liquid juice.

A third state of matter is gas. The steam coming out of this train has formed from water vapor, which is a gas.

The good science guide

Science is not only a collection of facts—it is the process that scientists use to gather information. Follow this good science guide to get the most out of each experiment.

• Carry out each experiment more than once. This prevents accidental mistakes skewing the results. The more times you carry out an experiment, the easier it will be to see if your results are accurate.

• Decide how you will write down your results. You can use a variety of different methods, such as descriptions, diagrams, tables, charts, and graphs. Choose the methods that will make your results easy to read and understand.

• Be sure to write your results down as you are doing the experiment. If one of the results seems very different from the others, it could be because of a problem with the experiment that you should fix immediately.

• Drawing a graph of your results can be very useful because it helps fill in the gaps in your experiment. Imagine, for example, that you plot time along the bottom of the graph and temperature up the side. If you measure the temperature ten times, you can put the results on the graph as dots. Use a ruler to draw a straight line through all the dots. You can now estimate what happened in between each dot, or measurement, by picking any point along the line and reading the time and temperature for that point from the sides of the graph.

• Learn from your mistakes. Some of the most exciting findings in science came from an unexpected result. If your results do not tally with your predictions, try to find out why.

• You should always be careful when carrying out or preparing any experiment, whether it is dangerous or not. Make sure you know the safety rules before you start working.

• Never begin an experiment until you have talked to an adult about what you are going to do.

ACTIVITY 1
STATES OF MATTER

*Matter is found in different forms called states. Each state
has different properties and uses. Understanding the different states
of matter is the first step to understanding how materials work.*

There are three basic kinds of matter: solid, liquid, and gas. Some materials can change from one kind to another. Solid, liquid, and gas are also called states of matter.

Substances like bricks and wood are solids. They keep their shape under normal temperature and pressure, unless something is done to them. That is why solids are used for making things that need to last, like buildings. In a solid the atoms are very close together and are held together very strongly by their bonds.

Liquids, such as water and milk, take the shape of whatever container they are put in. You see this every time you pour milk from a carton into a glass.

People have used solid materials, like this stone, to build with for thousands of years. The pyramids at Giza, Egypt (above), are more than 3,000 years old.

The atoms in a liquid are farther apart than those in a solid and are not held together as strongly.

Gases, such as air, also have no fixed shape. Unlike liquids, gases spread out to fill all the available space. The atoms in a gas are spread far apart and are held together very weakly. A gas can take up a lot of space, but under pressure the gas can be squeezed, or compressed, into a very small space. Scuba divers carry a supply of compressed air in tanks so that they can breathe underwater.

One way materials can change their state is by being heated or cooled. If you take a solid and add enough heat, the atoms will move apart, and the solid will turn into a liquid. Add more heat, and the atoms move even farther apart, and the liquid will turn into a gas. When you cool a gas, the atoms move together to become a liquid. Cool it even more, and it turns back into a solid.

CHANGING STATES

Sometimes when liquids are heated, they change permanently. For example, heating pancake batter turns it into a solid. This process cannot be reversed because the heat has rearranged the atoms in the pancake batter into new molecules. This type of change also happens when we burn coal or wood. The molecules in the coal or wood change into ash, which cannot turn back into wood.

The temperature at which a solid turns into a liquid is called the melting point. For water it is 32°F (0°C). The temperature at which a liquid turns into gas is the boiling point. The boiling point for water is 212°F (100°C). When water boils, the atoms are

Supercooled liquid

Glass is a surprising substance. Most people think it is a solid, but it is really a type of very thick liquid called a supercooled liquid. Look closely at an old window, and you will see that it is thicker at the bottom, where the glass has flowed down over time.

hot enough to move apart and become a gas—water vapor. Each liquid has its own boiling point.

When you freeze a liquid, the atoms move closer together, and the liquid turns into a solid. The temperature at which a liquid turns into a solid is called its freezing point. Water is unusual because it actually expands when it freezes (see page 11).

The freezing point of water is usually 32°F (0°C), but other materials can be added to change its freezing point. If you add salt, the water will not freeze until it is 5°F (−15°C). That is why people put salt on icy roads in winter. The salt stops rain from freezing into ice, and it also makes ice or snow melt to clear the road.

Three states of matter

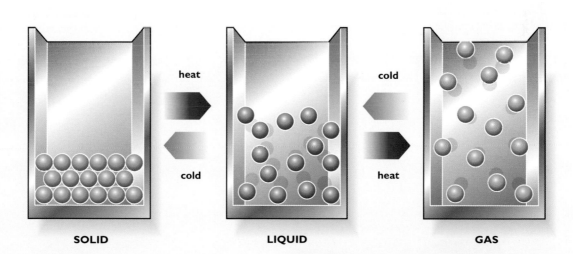

SOLID   **LIQUID**   **GAS**

Most of the matter in the universe is found in one of three states: solid, liquid, or gas. As you can see in the diagrams, the atoms in a solid are much closer together than in a liquid, and the atoms in a liquid are closer together than in a gas. Heating a solid causes the atoms to move apart and become a liquid, just as heating a liquid will make the atoms move even farther apart to become a gas. When the heat is removed, the atoms move closer together, and the gas turns back into a liquid. Remember: A gas will expand to fill all of the available space.

Making Ice Cream

Goals

1. **Learn to lower the temperature of ice.**
2. **Change the state of different materials to create new materials.**
3. **Make some tasty ice cream.**

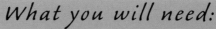

What you will need:

- *2 cups of milk or half-and-half*
- *1 sandwich-size Ziploc bag*
- *¼ cup of sugar*
- *2 teaspoons of chocolate sauce or vanilla extract*
- *4 cups of ice*
- *½ cup of salt*
- *1 large Ziploc freezer bag*
- *masking tape or duct tape*

1 Pour the milk or half-and-half into the small Ziploc bag, and add the sugar.

2 Add the chocolate sauce, and zip the bag closed.

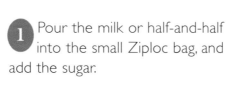

3 Squeeze the bag with your hand to mix the ingredients. Make sure they are well mixed.

(4) Put 2 cups of ice and ¼ cup of salt in the large bag, then another 2 cups of ice and ¼ cup of salt. Put the small bag inside the large bag, pushing it down into the ice so that it is partly covered in ice.

(5) Close and seal the large bag, and start shaking it back and forth and up and down. You might need to put on mittens! Keep shaking the bag for about 15 minutes.

Experiment with flavors

Make more exciting flavors of ice cream by adding crushed up candy bars to the milk just before you seal up the small bag. Use food coloring to make the ice cream more colorful.

(6) After the 15 minutes are over, open the bags, and enjoy your ice cream.

Troubleshooting

What if the ice cream doesn't freeze?

The first thing you should do is simply seal the bags up again and shake for a few more minutes. Or, you could make the ice cream using less milk, so that it will freeze faster. To do this, simply cut all the measurements in the recipe in half.

You could also try adding more ice and salt to the large bag, and stirring the ice and salt together to make sure the salt is well mixed with the ice.

FOLLOW-UP Making ice cream

You can test how salt lowers the freezing point of water in the following way. Take two plastic cups, and fill each one with ice. Measure the temperature in each cup with a thermometer. The temperature in both cups should be 32°F (0°C). Now pour a few tablespoons of salt into one cup, stir it around for a minute, then let it sit for a minute. Measure the temperature in both cups again. How much colder is the cup that contains the salt? You can chart the difference in temperature between the cups by taking a reading every minute for ten minutes. In which cup will the ice melt first?

A similar experiment can be done to find the freezing points of different liquids. Take three different liquids, such as dishwashing liquid, soda, and fruit juice. Put one cup of each liquid into a plastic bag, and seal it up, then put the bags into the freezer.

Check the liquids regularly, and write down how long it takes for each to form a solid.

Now try freezing the liquids using the mixture of salt and ice, as in the ice cream experiment. Do the liquids freeze faster this way? You can plot your results on another graph.

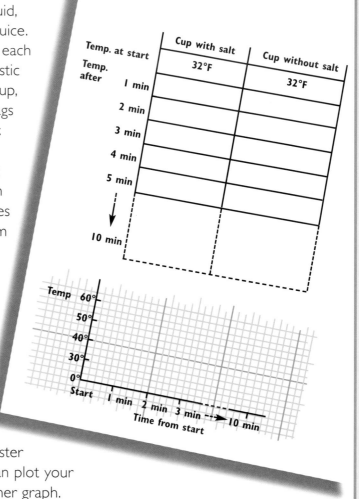

ANALYSIS

States of matter

After making your own ice cream, the first question you might have asked yourself is, "Why did I need to use the salt at all? After all, the ice cream in my freezer stays frozen without any salt."

The answer is that the temperature of water ice (a mixture of ice and water) is 32°F (0°C), but your freezer is colder. You can test this with two thermometers. Take one thermometer, and put it in the freezer. After an hour take a read-ing of the freezer's temperature. Place a second thermometer on an ice cube outside the freezer to measure the temperature of water ice. Compare the two readings—the one from the freezer should be colder.

In the main experiment adding salt to the water ice made it cold enough to freeze the ice cream. Water freezes at 32°F (0°C), but milk and sugar need to get colder than that to freeze. That is why you needed to add salt to the ice,

When people put salt on the roads in winter (left), it helps prevent ice forming. If the road is already icy, the salt will make the ice melt, because salt and water together do not freeze unless the temperature is lower than 32°F (0°C).

to make the ice as cold as your freezer—cold enough to freeze the ice cream. Remember that the freezing point of ice cream is lower than the freezing point of water. You have probably already realized that you can also make ice cream by simply leaving the milk mixture in your freezer—but without shaking the bag, the ice cream will not be very fluffy.

Ice cream is made when a mixture of milk, sugar, and flavoring freezes while being shaken or stirred. If just ice by itself was put around the milk mixture, then the mixture would not get cold enough to freeze. However, the combination of salt and water lowered the freezing point of ice to a temperature cold enough to make the ice cream freeze. Salt water freezes at a lower temperature than plain water.

When the salt molecules and the water molecules that make up the ice were put together, they formed a new substance—salt water, which has a lower freezing point than just water alone and will freeze your ice cream.

Below the ice

Water is a very strange substance. When most liquids freeze, their atoms move closer together, and the solid, frozen state takes up less space than the liquid state. However, when water freezes, it actually expands and takes up more space. The atoms in water move farther apart when water turns into ice.

Without this unusual property life might never have evolved in the oceans. Because water expands when it freezes, ice is lighter than liquid water. You prove this every time you drop an ice cube in a glass of water: The ice floats on the water because it is lighter. Ice in the ocean also floats, forming a kind of blanket that stops deeper water from getting cold enough to freeze. Thanks to this a huge variety of ocean life can live under the ice, even in the coldest parts of the planet. However, scientists think that if ice didn't float, the oceans could freeze solid, except for a thin layer of water at the surface, and very few organisms could survive there.

ACTIVITY 2
STRUCTURE OF CRYSTALS

Every material has a different structure. This structure gives a material its properties, such as color, hardness, smell, and shape. These properties also determine what each material can be used for.

Crystals are often embedded in rock. The rock above is from Durango, Mexico, and contains crystals of a mineral called rose quartz.

Look at something made of wood, and think about the following questions: What does the object look like? What does it feel like? What color is it? Now look at something made from metal, and ask yourself the same questions.

Both wood and metal are materials, but they look and feel very different. That is because wood and metal have different properties. A property is a description of a material—such as the way it looks or feels, its color or smell, or how soft and flexible it is. Every material can have hundreds of different properties. The properties allow us to tell different materials apart and help us know which material to use for a particular job.

For example, different rocks and minerals have different uses because of the different properties they each have. Marble is used for the outside of buildings and for statues because it can be polished to look beautiful. Chalk is very soft, but that makes it good for writing on blackboards and sidewalks. It also makes it easier to rub away or wash off.

One of the main things that determines the properties of a material is the material's chemical structure—the way its atoms are put together.

Crystals are materials that have a wide variety of properties. That is because each kind of crystal has a different structure. Many crystals formed deep underground inside molten rock—magma. When magma cools down, it solidifies to form solid rock, and crystals often grow inside it.

Diamond, quartz, emeralds, coal, and graphite (pencil "lead") are all crystals that form underground. Each of these crystals has its own distinctive properties. Diamond sparkles when it is cut, and when polished it is very hard, which is why diamond is used both for jewelry and also to cut things. Rubies and sapphires are very beautiful crystals that are also used for jewelry. Coal and graphite are made of the same atoms as diamond, but they have very different properties. Diamond is transparent, but coal and graphite are black. Coal burns well and so is used for fuel, while graphite is soft, so it is used as the "lead" inside pencils.

The atoms in a crystal are held together in what is called a lattice shape. This means that instead of being all jumbled up, the atoms are arranged very neatly into rows and columns. The rows are also arranged very neatly in one of 14 different patterns. The number of rows and columns, and the shape in which they are arranged, determines the properties of each type of crystal.

SOLUTIONS

As well as forming underground, crystals can develop in solutions. A solution is a kind of liquid. It forms when one substance, called a solute, dissolves in a liquid, such as water. Salt water, for example, is a solution made of salt (the solute) and water. When a solute dissolves in a solution, its atoms separate, and the solute seems to disappear.

If the water in a solution evaporates (turns into a gas), solute atoms stick together to form a crystal shape. This is how stalactites and stalagmites form. Salt flats in deserts form this way, too. Salt flats, stalactites, and stalagmites all have different properties because they are made of different materials.

Crystals are easy to make at home. In the following activity you will use a solution to make one kind of crystal and study its properties.

Crystal structure

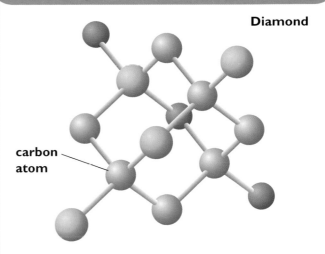

Diamond

carbon atom

Diamond and graphite are both made from carbon atoms, but they do not look the same or have the same properties. That is because the rows of carbon atoms are arranged differently. In diamond each carbon atom is rigidly connected to four other atoms, forming a very strong structure. In graphite, however, each carbon atom is connected to only three other atoms in a two-dimensional structure, so graphite forms flat, slippery sheets that make it soft.

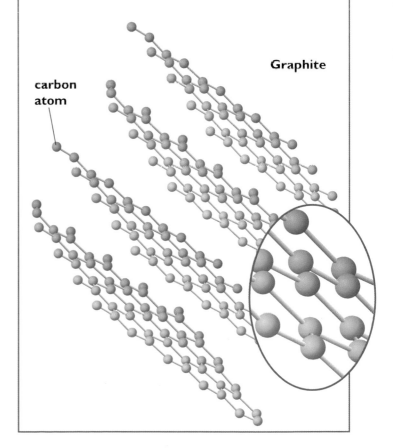

Graphite

carbon atom

Making Crystals

ACTIVITY

Goals

1. Make a solution from salt and water.
2. Study how solutions make crystals.
3. Discover different crystal shapes.
4. Grow your own "garden" of colorful and fluffy crystals.

What you will need:

- 2 tablespoons of salt
- 6 tablespoons of water
- rubber gloves
- 2 tablespoons of household ammonia
- foil pie plate
- food coloring
- 3–4 charcoal briquets (or small pieces of broken brick)

1 Lay out a sheet of newspaper to protect your work surface. Put 2 tablespoons of salt into a cup or container.

Safety tip

Ammonia can irritate your skin, so it is best to wear gloves when working with ammonia. Do not inhale or drink the ammonia.

2 Add 6 tablespoons of water to the salt. Stir the mixture until the salt has dissolved. Now, you have a solution.

3 Wearing gloves, add 2 tablespoons of ammonia to the salt-water solution.

4 Stir the solution briefly to mix the ingredients

Sugar crystal

You can make an edible crystal by mixing one cup of sugar in one cup of hot water. Stir the solution until the sugar has dissolved, and pour it into a clean glass jar.

Knot a thread in two places, leaving a space between the knots. Tie the thread to a pencil, and place the pencil over the jar so that the thread hangs in the solution. Make sure it does not touch the bottom of the jar.

Put the jar somewhere it will not be disturbed. After about a week you should have a large sugar crystal that you can eat.

5 Place the briquets in the foil pie plate.

6 Add some color by dropping food coloring onto the briquets in a few places.

7 Pour your salt solution over the briquets, but do not completely cover them.

8 Leave the dish outside on a window ledge, and wait for the crystals to grow. Over the next few days they will grow into a colorful crystal "garden" made of fluffy crystals.

FOLLOW-UP   Making crystals

You may want to experiment with the different ways that temperature affects the growth of crystals. To do this, make up two more trays like those in the main experiment, but put one in a hot place and one in a cold place. Compare how quickly the crystals grow, and look for any differences.

You can also try mixing different solutions. In one leave out the salt, and in a second leave out the ammonia. Now repeat the experiment, using different trays for each solution, and watch what happens.

You can make another kind of crystal by using alum, which you can buy from a pharmacy. Mix 4 tablespoons of alum in 1 cup of warm water, and pour it into a clean glass jar. Knot a thread in two places, leaving a space between the knots. Tie the thread around a pencil, and hang the thread in the jar, taking care not to let the thread touch the bottom of the jar. Put the jar somewhere no one will disturb it, and then watch what happens. Check the jar each day to see how fast the crystal grows and what shape it forms.

ANALYSIS
Structure of crystals

When you stirred the salt in the water, it formed a solution. The salt dissolved—it split up into separate atoms that spread throughout the water.

The charcoal soaks up the solution like a sponge. It also filters out any salt particles that are too big to move through the spaces in the coal. As the liquid on the surface of the charcoal evaporates, salt builds up and forms crystals. They grow larger as more and more salt is deposited. The ammonia helps dissolve the salt, and it also rearranges the salt atoms to make fluffy crystals. You should also see colored crystals in the places where you dropped food coloring. The food coloring dyed the salt, giving the crystals color.

Crystals also form when certain substances freeze. For example, when the water in a cloud freezes, it forms crystals of ice, or snowflakes (right and below). Snowflakes form quickly. They are easy to examine with a good magnifying glass.

Scientists study more complicated crystals by using x-rays. They are a bit like light rays, but they are invisible to the human eye. A beam of x-rays is shined through the crystal. The direction of the light beam is changed as it bounces off the atoms in the crystal. As the beam emerges, the x-ray makes a pattern. This pattern is a like a fingerprint—it contains clues that help scientists identify the atoms inside the crystal and figure out their arrangement.

ACTIVITY 3
EXTRACTING MATERIALS

Some materials are not found by themselves in a pure state but are mixed in with other substances. These materials have to be separated to purify them. We call this process extracting.

Many of the most valuable or useful materials are pure. Iron, for example, is a pure type of metal, and sugar is a pure type of food. Neither iron nor sugar occur as pure substances in nature—we have to take them out of the natural materials they are mixed with. This is called extraction.

Metals often exist in nature as ores—rocks that contain metals or other useful materials mixed in. Once an ore has been discovered, it is removed from the ground by mining so that the metal can be separated, or extracted, from the rock.

Iron is extracted from iron ore in a process called smelting. The iron ore is fed into a large fire called a blast furnace, along with coke (a type of coal) and limestone. Hot air is blown into the furnace to make the coke burn at extremely high temperatures. The rock in the ore burns away, and the impurities stick to the limestone, leaving the iron behind. The iron melts and flows to the bottom of the blast furnace, where it is poured out of a tap to cool and solidify.

If a useful material is dissolved in a solution, it can often be extracted by evaporation. The solution is heated or left to dry until all the liquid has evaporated (turned to gas), leaving the solid behind. Sugar is made this way from the sweet juice in sugarcane plants. Some materials can be extracted by crushing. Olive oil, for example, is made by crushing olives to release the edible oil inside them.

EXTRACTING SALT

One of the most common minerals is salt. We could not live without salt—our bodies need it to work properly. Before refrigerators were invented, salt was used to dry food so that it would last all winter. For thousands of years people have extracted

These rocks in Great Salt Lake, Utah, are covered in deposits of salt crystals left by evaporating water.

salt from seawater by simply leaving the water to evaporate in the sun. When all the water has evaporated, the salt is left behind. Today, most salt comes from "rock salt"—solid, underground salt that formed millions of years ago from evaporating seawater. Rock salt contains other materials besides salt, but we can extract the salt to purify it. We can do this in two stages: filtration and evaporation.

Filtering and Evaporation

Goals

1. **Learn the principles of filtration, evaporation, and extraction.**
2. **Purify salt by removing any impurities it contains.**

What you will need:

- ½ lb (227 g) rock salt
- water
- filter paper
  - bowl
  - scales
  - strainer
  - wooden spoon
  - heat source
  - saucepan

Hot water

The hotter the water, the more easily the salt will dissolve, but be careful when you are using hot water.

1 Crush the rock salt by putting it in a plastic bag and hitting it carefully with a rolling pin. Weigh the crushed salt, and write down its weight.

2 Pour the salt into the saucepan.

3 Add one cup of water to the salt, and heat it over low heat. Stir until most of the salt has dissolved, then let the liquid cool down.

4 Place the filter paper in a strainer over the bowl, and gently pour the mixture through the filter. Keep the filter paper and anything left on it. They are impurities.

5 Place the bowl in a warm place, like a windowsill in the sun, and let it sit for several days. Salt crystals should start to form as the water evaporates. These crystals are a much purer salt.

6 Weigh the crystals. Are they the same weight as the salt you started with?

Impurities

If the rock salt is impure, the impurities will form a brown layer on the filter paper. This is called residue. Don't worry about the residue; it will be purified from the salt.

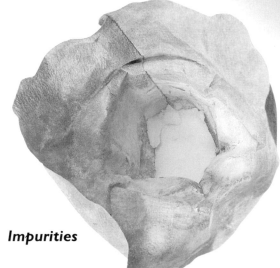

Impurities

Pure salt

FOLLOW-UP Filtering and evaporation

You might want to repeat your experiment using other crystal substances, such as sugar. You could also try using ready-mixed solutions, such as ink, to see what solids are left after evaporation.

You can test the impurities for iron by passing a magnet over the residue in the paper. Iron is magnetic, so any residue that sticks to the magnet contains iron. You can also

check for other metals in the residue by doing a flame test. You should only do this test in school as part of a science class or with your parents' help.

For the flame test you will need a bunsen burner (or another type of burner) and a nichrome wire, available at chemical or school supply stores. This test requires you to use a hot flame, so you must be very careful and only do it with an adult present.

Cut a length of wire about 4 inches (10cm) long, and push one end of the wire into a cork to make a handle. Open the air hole on the bunsen burner slightly, until the color has gone out of the flame.

Heat the nichrome wire in the flame for a few seconds to clean it, then let it cool. Dip the end of the wire into the residue, and then place it in the edge of the flame. Watch carefully to see if the flame changes color. If the flame turns blue, lead is present; a yellow flame means sodium is present; lilac is potassium; apple green is barium; blue-green is copper; and red shows the presence of calcium.

ANALYSIS
Extracting materials

In the experiment on the previous pages you used two processes, filtration and evaporation, to extract pure salt from rock salt, which is a mixture of salt and other (harmless) mineral impurities. Filtration and evaporation are common processes used to separate mixtures of different materials. Evaporation is also used to separate liquids with different boiling points.

First, you crushed the rock salt to make it easier to dissolve. Then, you dissolved the salt in water to make a solution. At this stage the salt and impurities were still together in the water.

In order to separate the salt from the impurities, you poured the solution through a filter. A filter catches large particles but lets tiny particles—such as separate atoms and molecules—pass straight through. The salt had split up into smaller particles when it dissolved, so it went through the filter along with the water. However, the impurities did not dissolve. They

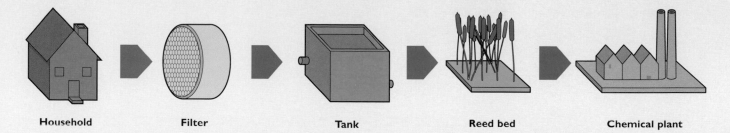

Household   Filter   Tank   Reed bed   Chemical plant

were still in the form of particles too big to pass through the filter paper.

After evaporation, which removed the water, you should have seen salt crystals form in the bowl. This salt was much purer than rock salt, but it was still not completely pure. It probably contained tiny flecks of impurities that were small enough to pass through the filter paper. It might also have contained small amounts of impurities that can dissolve in water.

WATER PURIFICATION

Filtration and evaporation are also commonly used to purify water. The water that comes into our homes is purified so that we can drink it. The waste water that leaves our homes also has to be purified before going back into rivers and seas. First, the waste water is passed through several different kinds of filters. It is then al-

Waste water from houses and other buildings is treated in a multistep process that involves filtration, the settling out of large material in tanks, letting plants remove impurities naturally, and finally, treatment with chemicals, after which it can be returned to rivers.

lowed to settle in tanks so that solids sink to the bottom. Smaller particles can be removed by passing the water through reed beds. The reeds naturally filter some impurities. The water is then treated chemically to kill any bacteria that might be living in it. Once clean, the water can be discharged into a river or even used again for some purposes.

Smelting iron ore

Iron is extracted from its ore by smelting in a blast furnace. The biggest blast furnaces can reach temperatures of 3500°F (1900°C) and make thousands of tons of iron in a single day. The blast furnace gets its name from the blast of hot air that heats up the raw materials—iron ore, limestone, and coke (a form of coal).

The melted iron sinks to the bottom of the furnace, where it runs out through a tap. When the limestone melts, it combines with the sand, clay, and stones in the ore to form a waste material called slag, which separates from the melted metal and floats on top of it. The slag is dumped in huge piles called slag heaps.

ACTIVITY 4
MOLDING AND SHAPING

Most of the familiar materials we use in our everyday lives have been made from substances that can be molded into many different shapes and sizes. There are many different ways to mold and shape materials.

Because different materials are made from different atoms and compounds, they must be shaped using different methods. A shaping method that works well on one type of material might not work well on another type of material.

Hard metals, such as iron, are molded into new objects by a process called casting. First, the metal is heated until it melts and turns into a liquid. The liquid metal is then poured into a mold and left to cool. As the metal hardens, it takes the shape of the mold. One traditional method of casting is sand casting. In sand casting a hollow mold is first made

Cheap, colorful plastic containers, like these at a market in Pujili, Ecuador, have taken the place of hand-made clay pots for most people around the world.

out of sand and clay. Molten metal is poured into the mold and left to cool and solidify. When the metal has cooled, the mold is broken open with a hammer to free the new object.

Metal wire is made by heating a metal rod until it is soft enough to pull through a small hole. This is done several times, through smaller and smaller holes, until the wire is very thin.

To shape softer metals like gold, the metals are either melted and poured into molds or heated until soft, and then the softened metals are hammered into shape with small hammers.

SHAPING GLASS

Glass is made by melting silica, the main mineral found in sand. One ancient method of shaping glass that is still used today is to use air to blow hot, liquid glass into shape. Glassblowers do this by putting a blob of hot liquid glass onto the end of a hollow pipe and blowing into the pipe.

Early windows made of thin, flat glass were made by blowing a bubble of glass, flattening it, and then attaching it to a rod called a pontil. The window maker then spun the pontil around as fast as possible to make the soft glass spread out into a flat circle. The ancient Romans made sheets of glass by waiting for the hot liquid to cool slightly and then using tools to stretch it out. But none of these methods made a clear glass of an even thickness.

Today windows are made by a method called the float glass process. The glass is heated to make it more flexible, then it passes through a set of rollers, which give it an even thickness. From there it enters

These workers are casting gold bars. The gold was a by-product of copper smelting at a smelting plant in Magna, Utah.

a float tank, where it floats on top of a pool of liquid metal. The floating glass forms a very smooth layer. This would shatter if it cooled down suddenly, so it is allowed to cool very slowly. Finally, a diamond-tipped blade cuts the glass into sheets.

Blowing glass

This man is shaping glass by using a traditional method called glassblowing. He is blowing through a long pipe to make the blob of molten glass at the end expand like a bubble. By turning the pipe and controlling the way that he blows, the glassblower can make different shapes of glass. In ancient times this was the only way of making glass containers.

After he has shaped the glass, the glassblower can color it by rolling it through different mineral powders and pigments while it is still hot. Glass objects made by blowing need to be cooled slowly in an oven. Otherwise, they would crack when they meet the cool air.

Most glass objects are now made by machine, but glassblowing is still used to make ornaments and scientific instruments.

Molding Sugar Glass

Goals

1. **Study an ancient way of making and molding glass**
2. **Learn how to shape materials by using heat.**
3. **Make your own sugar glass.**

What you will need:

- *1 tablespoon of butter*
- *nonstick baking tray*
- *1 cup of sugar*
- *nonstick saucepan*
- *1 tablespoon of water*
- *heat source*
- *wooden spoon*

1 Spread the butter on the baking tray, and place it in the refrigerator to cool.

2 Pour the sugar into the saucepan with 1 tablespoon of water, and heat it gently at a low temperature.

3 Stir the sugar slowly to keep it from burning. After a few minutes the sugar will turn into a brown liquid.

Molding a box

Try another method for molding sugar glass by pouring the liquid sugar into a plastic, heat-proof container and leaving it to cool in the refrigerator. When it is cool, remove the sugar, and see what shape it has made.

4 Pour the molten sugar onto the cold baking tray, and leave it to cool. The butter will melt, but it will form a layer between the heavier sugar syrup and the tray, and will keep the sugar from sticking to the tray.

Safety tip

Hot sugar can burn. Do not do this activity without an adult to help you.

5 When it is cold, carefully peel the sugar-glass pane from the baking tray.

Different shapes

You can mold the sugar glass into different shapes, but it might take some practice. Make a pane of sugar glass the same way as in the main experiment. Then, when the sugar pane has cooled, but while it is still soft, you can shape it by draping it over a bowl or a glass that you have coated in butter. When the sugar glass sets hard, it should hold the shape of the bowl or glass. Make small "sugar bowls" to serve ice cream in at your next party. When your guests have finished the ice cream, tell them that they can eat the bowl!

FOLLOW-UP Molding sugar glass

Many of the materials that people mold and shape are soft solids that harden when they are baked or left to dry. One example is clay, which people have used for thousands of years. Clay is common in nature and easy to shape, so it may have been one of the first materials that people used for making objects.

Clay is made up of very small crystals of potassium, aluminum, and silicon, combined with air and water. The crystals slide over each other when lots of water is present, making the clay soft and flexible. That is why clay has to be kept wet while it is being molded. Wet clay can be shaped by turning it on a potter's wheel, or it can be pushed into a mold. The first bricks were probably made from a mixture of clay and straw that was packed into rectangular molds.

After it has been shaped, the clay object is left to dry at room temperature or outside in the sun, which allows the water to evaporate. When clay dries, the crystals inside it stick together, which makes the clay shrink and become hard.

After drying, clay objects are often baked in an oven called a kiln at temperatures of up to 3092°F (1700°C). This is called firing. Firing makes the molecules in clay move closer together, and the object becomes harder. After fired clay has cooled, there is no longer enough room between the clay molecules for water molecules to reenter, so the object will stay hard even if it gets wet again.

Many people use clay pots for storage and cooking. These small, unglazed pots in Himachel Pradesh, India, are drying in the sun.

Cookie dough is similar to clay. Raw dough is soft, but it hardens when baked. You can study the way clay is shaped with the following edible experiment.

1

What you will need:
½ cup of soft margarine
½ cup of sugar
bowl
fork or spoon for stirring
1 egg
1 cup of plain flour
pinch of salt
baking tray

1 Beat the margarine and sugar together in a bowl. Crack the egg into the mixture, and stir to mix everything well. Next, add the flour and salt, and stir until it forms a dough.

2 Break off small pieces of the dough, and mold them into pot shapes with your hands. Bake them in a 375°F (190°C) oven for 15 minutes. When they have cooled down, fill the cookie pots with jam, chocolate, or peanut butter, and eat them.

You can also try other molding methods to decorate the cookie pots. Take some of the cookie mix, and put it in a garlic crusher. Press the crusher to make skinny dough wires, and use them to decorate the pots before you bake them.

ANALYSIS
Molding and shaping

Glass, even the glass in windows, is a liquid. At room temperature glass is an extremely thick liquid that moves very, very slowly—over hundreds of years. It is much too thick and stiff for us to mold or shape; but when glass is heated, it gets softer and becomes easier to mold.

Sugar is a solid, but we can turn it into a liquid by heating it until it melts. When sugar melts, it turns into a thick, sticky liquid similar to molten glass. Because the bonds in the liquid sugar are only loosened a little bit, the sugar, like glass, can be stretched and shaped.

If you tried to shape the cooling sugar glass by rolling it with a rolling pin or stretching it with tongs, then you would have experienced some of the same problems that the Romans did when they tried to make glass windows. It is very difficult to make glass panels with an even thickness and clarity.

MOLDING COOKIES

The cookie-making follow-up activity demonstrated that soft materials can be shaped and molded in a variety of different ways.

Like clay, dough is easier to work with when it is damp because water allows the dough molecules to move around easily. Baking the cookies causes changes in the dough that are similar to the changes that happen when clay is fired. The oven heats up the water inside the dough and makes it evaporate, so the dough dries out, and the dough molecules can no longer move around easily. The heat also causes chemical changes in the egg and the flour that make the dough molecules fuse together. These changes are permanent, so you cannot turn cookies back into dough just by making them wet.

Try to think of other types of foods that we can mold and shape, and then use heat, chemicals, or cold to make them keep their shape.

CUTTING AND SHAPING

Some materials have to be cut into pieces or made into a certain shape before we can use them. There are thousands of different tools that people use to cut and shape materials.

🔲 *Two young men saw lumber with a two-handed saw at their village along the Mekong River in Luang Prabang Province, Laos.*

Many materials, such as metals, are produced in large amounts, but often only a small amount is needed. Before the material can be used, it has to be cut into pieces the right size. To do this, we use special tools for cutting and shaping.

There are lots of different cutting and shaping tools because there are so many different types of materials. Can you imagine cutting a banana with a blow torch or cutting steel with a butter knife? For every type of material there are certain tools that do the job better than any other.

Not all materials have to be cut to size. Soft materials can sometimes be broken up by hand, and liquids can simply be poured out in the right amount. However, hard materials usually have to be cut with some kind of blade. Cutting tools include knives, axes, saws, blowtorches, and lasers. To get rid of the rough edges after cutting, people also use smoothing tools like sandpaper and files.

The earliest cutting tools were made from pieces of flint, which is a type of stone. People made flint tools by using a hard rock to chip away at a piece of flint to create the blade. This is called knapping. The earliest flint tools were hand-held and were probably used for cutting meat or stripping the skin from dead animals. Later, people attached handles made from antlers or branches.

When people discovered how to shape metals, they created stronger and sharper cutting tools from copper and iron. The first saws were made out of copper in Egypt in about 1500 B.C. Copper is not a very strong metal, and the saws could only cut if they were pulled backward.

Modern saws have two sets of teeth: One set cuts when the blade is pushed forward, and a second set cuts when the blade is pulled back. The materials that a saw can cut depend on the size of its teeth. A fine-tooth hacksaw can cut metal, while saws with larger teeth are used on wood. In 1947 the first hand-held chainsaw was invented. It could cut through wood four times faster than a handsaw.

The most common way of cutting materials is to use a sharp knife. But, if a material is soft, it can be cut and shaped with some surprising tools.

Cutting tools

Different cultures have developed different tools for cutting and shaping because each culture needs to cut and shape different materials.

6 inches (15cm)

The knife in the top right was probably invented by the Inuit people, who use the curved blade for removing the skin and blubber from seals and whales. Similar knives are also used in Japan for cutting vegetables and herbs into small pieces.

The cutting tool at the bottom right is a scythe. Its long, curved blade is the perfect shape and size for cutting down tall stalks of wheat or other grains. Scythes have been used for cutting grain and making hay for thousands of years.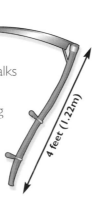

4 feet (1.22m)

Think about the cutting tools that different cultures use. Can you tell from the shape of each tool what materials it is used to cut?

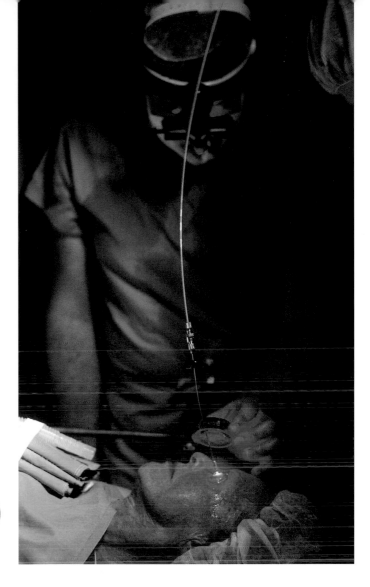

Surgeons use lasers to make very fine cuts in certain parts of the body, such as the eye. Lasers do less damage to delicate tissue than metal blades.

CUTTING WITHOUT BLADES

A sharp blade is not the only way to cut materials. One way of cutting wood, fabric, stone, and even metal is to use a fast jet of water. The water comes out of a machine that controls the jet very carefully, allowing precise cutting.

Another way of cutting is to use a beam of light called a laser. Laser beams are used for precise cutting because they are very thin and perfectly straight. They cut by producing heat. Surgeons sometimes use lasers during operations. The heat seals the wound as it cuts.

Heat is also used for cutting metal. A tool called a blowtorch produces a very hot, pointed flame that melts metal only where the flame touches.

Shaping Materials

Goals

1. **Study the properties of materials by exploring how to cut them.**
2. **Learn about different tools used for cutting.**

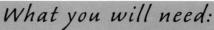

What you will need:

- *plastic straw*
- *potato*
- *piece of wood*
- *different sandpapers*
- *thread*
- *a handful of clay*
- *¼ cup of water*
- *1 cup of plain flour*
- *¼ cup of salt*

1 Hold a raw potato in one hand and the drinking straw in the other hand. Try to cut off a piece of potato with the straw.

2 Now put your thumb over one end of the straw, and stab it into the potato. What happens?

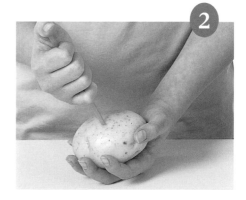

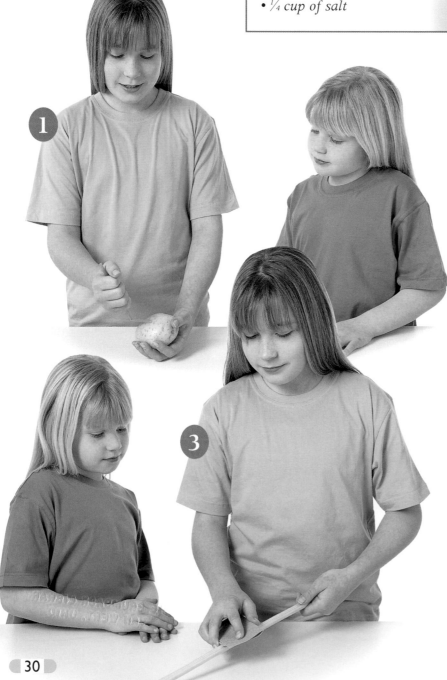

3 Use a few different types of sandpaper to shape a piece of wood. Which type of sandpaper makes the wood smoothest? Which type shapes the wood fastest?

4 You can cut clay with a thread by wrapping the thread in a loop around a blob of clay and pulling the loop tight.

Oh coconuts!

Coconuts are covered in a thick, fibrous husk that ancient people found impossible to cut with knives. Instead, they stuck sharpened sticks in the ground and opened the coconuts by banging them onto the sticks until they cracked. This method is still used today. At the base of many coconut trees on Pacific islands you can find sharp sticks poking up out of the ground; they are used for husking and opening the nuts.

5 Put the flour in a bowl, and try to make it into a shape. It will be impossible to make any shape except for a mound.

6 If you add the salt and water to the flour, you can make a dough that will hold any shape you want. Dry the dough in a warm oven to make it hold the shape permanently. You can even paint the baked dough to make an ornament.

FOLLOW-UP — Shaping materials

Once you have tried different methods and different tools for cutting and shaping some materials, study the edges of the material you cut or shaped. Is it a clean cut, or does it have rough edges? Think about what other materials could be cut or shaped with your tools and what other nonsharp household objects you could use as cutting or shaping tools.

Make a list of cutting and shaping tools you use around the house every day. Which ones are sharp, and which ones are not?

Sharpness is not the only property that makes a tool good at cutting. Another important property is hardness. Scientists rate the hardness of minerals using a system called the Mohs' scale. Any mineral on the scale can scratch all the minerals with lower numbers.

The minerals on the Mohs' scale are not usually found around the house, but you can experiment with the alternatives in the table below. To rate the hardness of a material, such as wood or plastic, on the Mohs' scale, find out which of the household objects in the table can scratch it.

Mohs' scale	Mineral	Household equivalent
1	Talc	Chalk
2	Gypsum	Fingernail
3	Calcite	Bronze coin
4	Flourite	Iron nail
5	Apetite	Glass
6	Feldspar	Penknife blade
7	Quartz	Steel file
8	Topaz	Sandpaper
9	Corundum	No replacement
10	Diamond	No replacement

ANALYSIS — Cutting and shaping

Sharp blades are not the only tools that are useful for cutting. Sometimes it is better to use another tool, but the choice of tool depends on the material you are cutting. While a blade works well on softer materials, a saw or something abrasive, such as sandpaper, is best for harder materials. You might have noticed that the smoother sandpaper was best for smoothing the wood, while the rougher sandpaper shaped the wood the fastest.

A wire or thread can work just as well as a knife to cut soft materials. That is because a wire is as thin as the cutting edge of a knife, so when it is pulled tight, it can be just as sharp.

Powders, like flour, are too dry to stick together, so you cannot shape them into a single object. But, if you add the right amount of water to most powders, they become sticky and can be made into different shapes. Flour contains protein, which gets very sticky when it is

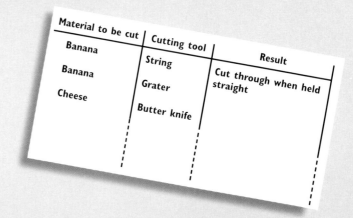

Material to be cut	Cutting tool	Result
Banana	String	Cut through when held straight
Banana	Grater	
Cheese	Butter knife	

🔵 *You might want to record the results of your experiments in a chart like this one.*

wet, so it is particularly good for shaping. In our experiment we added salt to the flour to make it harder once it became dry.

The next time you have to cut something, think carefully about the tool that you use—are you always using the best tool for the job?

ATTACHING MATERIALS

One way of making materials useful is to attach two or more of them together. How we do this depends on the structure of each material.

There are many different ways of attaching materials together. Before metal nails were invented, people joined pieces of timber together by hammering hard wooden pegs into holes in the timber joints. Clothes were made by sewing animal skins together using bone needles and sinews (tough fibers that attach muscles to bones) for thread.

Nails were first used around 3500 B.C. Made from copper, they were very soft. Later, iron and steel were used to make much stronger nails.

Pieces of metal can be joined together by welding. Welding uses heat to melt a small area of each metal. The two pieces are then stuck together and harden into a single solid piece. In the past, blacksmiths used large furnaces to carry out welding. Today welders use blowtorches—gas burners that produce a very powerful flame.

A protective helmet shields this welder from flying sparks as he welds two metals together in a factory in Saskatchewan, Canada.

STICKING TOGETHER

We use glues, or adhesives, to stick lots of different materials together. Glues are usually liquids that feel sticky to the touch. When they come in contact with the air, they harden and turn into a solid that bonds objects together.

The ancient Romans made glues by mixing resin with beeswax or bitumen (a type of tar). Resin is a sticky liquid that seeps out of cuts made in tree trunks. The Romans used their glues to attach pieces of wood together in ships. Wood glues fill the tiny pores and crevices in wood and bond wooden surfaces together strongly when they set.

Other early glues were made by boiling the hides and bones of animals to release a substance called protein. Animal protein is very sticky and makes a good glue. Egg whites and milk, which both come from animals and so contain animal protein, are still used as glue in many art-and-craft projects, such as sticking very thin papers together. Another good natural glue is starch, which comes from plants like rice and potatoes. Glues made from starch, egg white, and milk are not waterproof, so they cannot be used for joining materials that might get wet later.

Many modern glues are made of artificial chemicals and are very strong. The activity on the next page produces a natural animal-protein glue that was first used by the ancient Egyptians.

Milk Glue

ACTIVITY

Goals

1. Learn ways to bond different materials together.
2. Make a natural glue.
3. Experiment with mixing two materials to create a third, useful material.

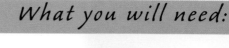

What you will need:

- 2 cups of milk
- 1 teaspoon of baking soda
- $\frac{1}{3}$ cup of vinegar
- saucepan
- strainer
- glass bowl
- wooden spoon
- 3 tablespoons of water

1 Pour the milk into the saucepan, and add the vinegar. Heat the milk gently until lumps start to form. Do not bring the milk to the boil.

2 Leave the milk to cool. As it cools, the mixture should separate further, until you have a large lump of material with a rubbery texture covered by a yellowish liquid.

3 Pour the mixture through a strainer, and throw the liquid away.

Safety tip

Do not use any kind of heat without an adult present. It is safest if you heat the mixture slowly and use a large saucepan.

4 Add the baking soda to the rubbery milk solid.

5 Add the water and stir the mixture well. The baking soda will react with the protein in the milk to form a glue.

Edible glue

You can make an edible glue, to use when you are making gingerbread houses or other sweets. Mix together three egg whites, 1 pound (0.45kg) of powdered sugar, and ½ teaspoon of cream of tartar. There are two important ingredients that make this glue sticky: egg whites, which are made of an animal protein, and sugar, which we all know is sticky stuff.

Troubleshooting

What if the glue is too watery and not sticky enough?

Different kinds of milk will produce different amounts of milk solid when heated with vinegar. Whole milk will produce the most milk solid.

If your glue is too watery and not sticky enough, you may need to make another batch using slightly less water. You could also try increasing the amount of baking soda that you add to the milk solid.

6 Try gluing pieces of paper or other objects together with your milk glue.

FOLLOW-UP   Milk glue

After you have made the glue, use it to stick different materials together. Use a chart or table to record which materials stick together the best, and which materials do not stick together at all with the milk glue.

You might also want to test whether the milk glue works under water. To do this, place the objects you have stuck together in a bowl of water, and leave them for 5 minutes. You could record the results from your experiments in a table like the one shown on the right.

You can make another simple glue by mixing a cup of flour or corn flour with about ⅓ cup of water. Make some of this corn-flour glue, and test it to find out whether it works better than the milk glue, and what materials it works best on. Try gluing two materials together with the milk glue, and then two more pieces of the same materials together with the corn-flour glue. Then put both pairs of the objects under water. What happens?

The milk solid that you collected with the strainer is used in India to make candies. Instead of adding baking soda, Indian cooks add sugar and food coloring and form the candies into different shapes.

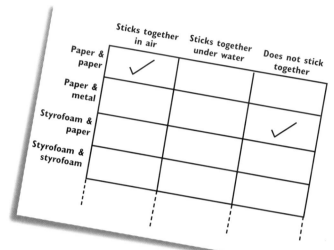

	Sticks together in air	Sticks together under water	Does not stick together
Paper & paper	✓		
Paper & metal			
Styrofoam & paper			✓
Styrofoam & styrofoam			

This is one type of chart that you can make to record the results of your experiments with milk glue.

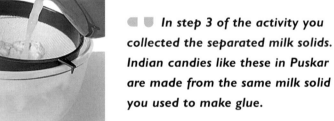

In step 3 of the activity you collected the separated milk solids. Indian candies like these in Puskar are made from the same milk solid you used to make glue.

ANALYSIS
Attaching Materials

When you heated the milk and vinegar, the animal protein separated out as milk solids, leaving behind a yellowish liquid called whey. The vinegar was left in the whey, not in the protein. When you added baking soda to the milk solids, it caused a chemical reaction that made the milk protein turn sticky. This milk glue is one of the oldest known forms of glue.

You can also make glue from starch, an edible substance found in foods like flour, potatoes, and rice. Starch gets sticky when it is wet and even stickier when it is cooked. You can see this the next time you eat mashed potatoes, which have a lot of starch in them—the cooked potatoes are much stickier than uncooked potatoes. You might have used starch glue if you have ever made papier-mâché. This kind of glue is not waterproof, though. You would have noticed this the last time you washed the dishes after a meal with mashed potatoes—the potatoes stop sticking when they get wet.

Natural glues, like milk glue or starch glue, work because they get inside the tiny holes on the surface of objects and then harden, forming a strong bond that links the two materials. But natural glues do not work well on very smooth surfaces like metal. To stick these things together, we need artificial glues.

ARTIFICIAL GLUES

Most glues we use today are made from artificial chemicals. They dry quickly and form very strong bonds. Some of the fastest glues are called superglues and set in seconds. Superglue is a resin made from oil. When it comes into contact with water, its small molecules join together to form longer, sticky molecules called polymers. Superglues will stick skin together because of the moisture on skin, and some superglues have been used in surgery to seal wounds.

Solvent glues are also artificial. A solvent is any substance that can dissolve other materials to make a solution. For example, water is a solvent that can dissolve sugar. Solvent glues contain a solid dissolved in a liquid. After the glue is spread, the solvent evaporates (turns to gas), leaving the solid behind. The glue on the back of some stamps is a solvent glue, but it's not poisonous, so it is safe to lick.

Papier-mâché

Making papier-mâché objects, like the colorful bowls above, is a popular craft. You might have made papier-mâché objects in an art project, but you may not have realized that, even though papier-mâché uses only paper and water, it also involves a type of natural glue.

Most paper is made from trees, and trees, like all plants, contain starch. Plants use starch to store energy. When starch gets wet, it forms a type of glue; but when it gets too wet, the glue washes away in water. That is why water ruins papier-mâché, and why mashed potatoes are easier to clean off plates if you soak them first.

ACTIVITY 7
CHANGING COLOR

One of the most common ways of changing materials is to change their color. People have been doing this for thousands of years. The most usual way of changing the color of materials is to dye them.

Some of the first dyes that people used were made from plants. Cabbage water, for instance, produces a green color, while onion skins were once used to give fabric a tan color. In the time of the ancient Romans some people in Britain colored their skin blue using woad, a dye made from plants.

Painters added minerals and dried ingredients called pigments to their paints, and by the 18th century a wide range of colors was available. Some of these dried pigments came from strange sources. Black pigment came from soot or from ground-up Egyptian mummies, for example, and red came from

🔲 *These trays in a market in Pushpatinah, Nepal, contain brightly colored tikka powder, which local people use for dyeing fabrics.*

the bodies of tiny insects that live on prickly pear cacti. White pigment was made from powdered lead, and yellow came from dried cow's urine.

Many pigments were very expensive. Lapis lazuli is a rare and precious stone that was ground into a fine powder to make a beautiful, bright blue color. Statues or portraits that contained this pigment were very expensive.

ARTIFICIAL DYES

In 1856 a British scientist created the first artificial dye. William Henry Perkin was trying to create an artificial form of quinine, the drug used to cure malaria. Instead, he made a black, sticky mess. When he tried to clean up the mess with alcohol, it produced a beautiful, light-purple color. He put some of this purple chemical on fabric and found that the fabric absorbed the color. Perkin called his dye mauveine. The color it produced—mauve—became very popular, and for the next decade it was the fashionable color to be seen wearing.

Many of the pigments we use today are artificial chemicals, and they can turn up in surprising places. Processed ham, for example, is naturally gray, but ham makers add food coloring to turn it pink. Margarine and some types of butter would be white if yellow food coloring were not added.

The dyes we use to color clothes and fabrics work in different ways. Some work only on natural fabrics like cotton and wool, while others are used for artifical fabrics, such as nylon. Many dyes need an extra chemical called a fixer to make them stick

In the city of Fez in Morocco people use large pools of dye to color leather and natural fabrics.

to the fabric, otherwise they wash off in water. Vat dyes are colorless and only become colored when the dyed fabric is exposed to the air. Denim gets its blue color from a vat dye called indigo.

The dyeing process

In some parts of the world people make patterned fabrics by carefully painting dye onto fabrics by hand. However, most of the clothes and fabrics that we wear are colored in a different way. Instead of dyeing fabrics after they have been woven, clothes factories dye the threads the clothes are made from. A weaving machine then combines the threads to make fabrics with colorful patterns. Most thread is dyed on a conveyor belt, which allows huge volumes of thread to be dyed continuously. The process shown below can be used for dyeing all kinds of fibers, from natural threads such as silk and cotton to artificial fibers, like polyester and nylon.

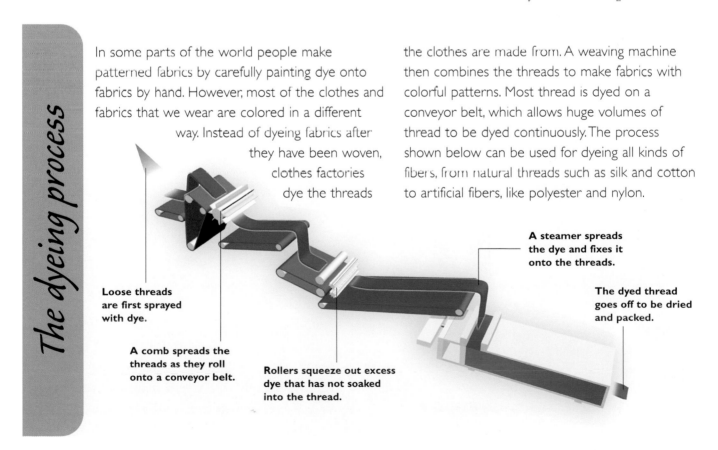

Loose threads are first sprayed with dye.

A comb spreads the threads as they roll onto a conveyor belt.

Rollers squeeze out excess dye that has not soaked into the thread.

A steamer spreads the dye and fixes it onto the threads.

The dyed thread goes off to be dried and packed.

Vegetable Dye

Goals

1. **Make a natural vegetable dye.**

2. **Learn about ancient methods of coloring fabric with dyes.**

3. **Use one material to change the appearance of another material.**

What you will need:

- *grater*
- *fresh, raw beets*
- *large bowl*
- *large saucepan*
- *water*
- *white cotton fabric*
- *long-handled wooden spoon*
- *rubber kitchen gloves*
- *newspaper*

Avoid beet stains

Beets can stain your hands and clothes, so it is best to wear old clothes and rubber kitchen gloves for this activity.

1 Grate three or four beets, and put them into the saucepan with a quart (about 1 liter) of water.

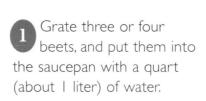

2 With an adult helping, boil the liquid, and let it simmer for half an hour. Make sure the water level stays the same by adding more water if necessary.

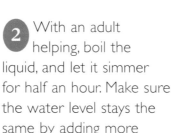

Safety tip

Never heat water without an adult's help, and always be extra careful when working with hot water. Use a long-handled wooden spoon or tongs to put the cotton in the water, to stir it around, and to take it out. Don't use an aluminum saucepan because the dye will stain it. Use a nonaluminum pan, or use an old pan that is okay to ruin.

3 Turn off the heat. Carefully put the cotton in the hot water, and leave it for 15 minutes.

4 Using a long-handled wooden spoon, stir the cotton around to make sure it is completely wet. Then leave it to cool down.

5 Once the water has cooled, after about an hour, take the cotton out. Be careful! The water and the cloth may still be hot.

6 Rinse the cotton in a bowl of warm water.

Troubleshooting

What if some parts of the fabric don't change color?

Dyes made from beets or other vegetables are natural dyes and will only stain natural fabrics, like cotton and wool.

If your cotton contains any stitched hems or buttonholes, the stitches will stay white if they are made of artificial fabrics, like polyester or nylon.

7 Hang the cotton to dry, with the newspaper on the floor below to catch drips. Leave the cotton overnight. You should now have a piece of colored fabric.

FOLLOW-UP   Vegetable dye

There are lots of foods that you can use as dyes. Try coffee, tea, grated carrots, or KoolAid, for instance.

Although cotton absorbs the beet dye well, the dye may not stay in the fabric. If you wash the cotton, keep it separate from clothes because the dye might run and stain them.

To prevent dye from running, you need to "fix" it. Fixers are chemicals that hold dye onto fabric and make the color more permanent. Natural fixers include salt, alum, vinegar, and even urine.

To fix beet dye, you need to repeat the activity with a new piece of cotton. You will need two new items: cream of tartar and a chemical called alum, which is sold in pharmacy stores. Ask an adult to help you make the fixer, and remember to wear rubber gloves when handling chemicals. Do not drink the chemicals, and try to avoid splashing when adding water.

Weigh the cotton, then wash and rinse it. For each half pound (225g) of cotton mix 0.3 ounces (10g) of alum, 1 tablespoon of cream of tartar, and 4 pints (2 liters) of hot water in a pan. Put the cotton in the pan, and simmer for an hour, keeping the pan covered.

Leave the pan to cool overnight. With rubber gloves carefully take out the cotton, and rinse it thoroughly in water. Clean up any spilled chemicals. Let the cotton drain, and then put it in a pan of beet dye as before. When the dyeing is finished, leave the cotton to dry in a dark place.

The final color depends on how much dye you use, whether you treat the cotton with fixer, and whether you give it an afterbath.

You can change the color of a dyed fabric by giving it an afterbath. Vinegar, lemon juice, and baking soda make good afterbaths. Experiment with an afterbath by mixing ¼ cup of one of these ingredients with a quart (1 liter) of water. After dyeing the fabric, soak it in the afterbath for 5 minutes, and hang it to dry.

ANALYSIS   Changing color

White light is a mixture of different colors. When white light strikes an object, some colors are absorbed, and the rest are reflected. The reflected colors are the ones we see.

The cotton in your experiment turned red because the molecules in the beets that reflect red light dissolved in water and then stuck to the fabric. If you washed the cotton later, you might have seen the red color run out into the water because there was nothing holding it in place. Adding a fixer, such as alum, to the cotton before dyeing helps the fabric hold onto the color molecules for longer.

Natural dyes, like dyes made from plants, will only dye natural fabrics, such as cotton, silk, or wool. Artificial fabrics, like nylon and polyester, have to be dyed with artificial dyes.

Another way of coloring fabrics is to print pictures or other patterns on them with ink. In modern factories, printing machines transfer colored patterns onto large rolls of fabric as the fabric slides through the machine. The printing is done by rollers that have a design cut onto them. Each roller passes through a trough containing colored ink and then transfers this ink to the fabric. Fabrics with very complex patterns can have as many as 16 rollers applying the color. The inks dry as the fabric comes off the final roller and passes through an oven.

OTHER USES FOR DYES

Dyes and pigments are added to a very wide variety of materials to give them color. Paints, for example, are made from a mixture of colored pigment and a special fixer, called a binder, that holds the pigment in the paint.

Cosmetics also contain pigments. In ancient Egypt women used a natural pigment called kohl to blacken their hair, eyebrows, and eyelashes. Kohl is made from a naturally occuring type of lead called galena. Today's cosmetics use a wide range of pigments and dyes, both natural and artificial.

Some sea animals use natural pigments for self-defense. The cuttlefish sprays black ink at its attackers to confuse them while it escapes. If you buy a fresh cuttlefish, you can remove its ink sac and use the ink to write messages.

A woman in Antigua, Guatemala, weaves dyed threads into a colorful cloth in a traditional pattern.

Colored glass

In the 11th and 12th centuries people began to color glass by adding minerals to the liquid glass as it was being made. Copper oxide gave glass a ruby red color, cobalt made it blue, iron oxide produced green glass, and alumina and phosphates make glass milky. Artists used the colored glass to create stained glass windows, like the one above in Jodhpur Fort, India.

Chemicals can change other properties of glass beside its color. Ovenproof cooking dishes and laboratory test tubes are made from glass containing a chemical called boron oxide. This chemical makes the glass able to stand high temperatures without cracking. Normally, glass shatters into sharp pieces, but the glass in car windows is made by cooling liquid glass rapidly with jets of air. Car windows shatter into lots of tiny pieces, which are less likely to cause injury.

ACTIVITY 8
ARTIFICIAL MATERIALS

Artificial materials are all around us and make our lives easier. The most common artificial materials are plastics, which are made from very long chains of molecules. Find out more about these amazing materials.

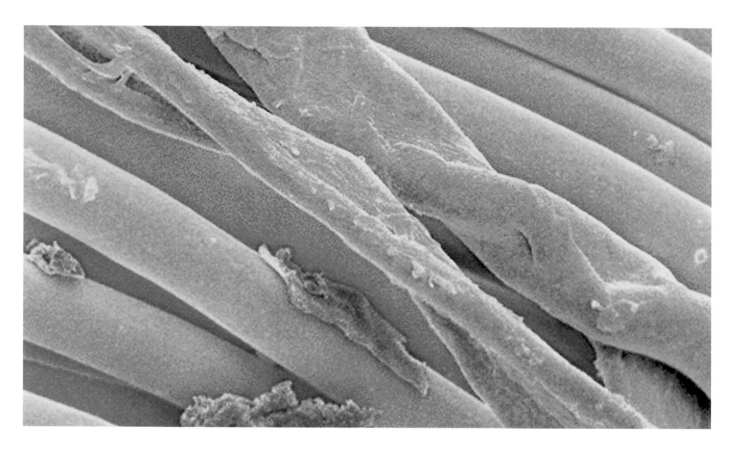

Think what life would be like without plastics. How many objects in your home are made out of plastic, and how many plastic objects do you use each day? If you check the labels inside your clothes, you might discover that they are made of plastic, too—polyester and nylon are types of artificial thread made of plastic.

Plastics belong to a class of materials called polymers. The molecules of a polymer are giant chains made up of smaller units repeated over and over. One of the reasons polymers are so useful is because the long molecules can fit together either loosely or tightly, producing materials with different properties. You can see how this works by com-

● *This closeup shows fibers of an artificial fabric (orange) and fibers of cotton (green), a natural material. The artificial threads are much smoother.*

paring a plastic bag and a plastic chair. They are both made of polymer molecules, but the molecules in the chair are held together more tightly, making the chair stiff enough to sit on. The molecules in the bag are held together loosely, which makes the bag easy to bend and fill with things.

Polymers are also common in nature. Hair, rubber, wood, and cotton are all made of natural polymers, for example. Many natural polymers are very useful materials, but plastics are sometimes better.

Plastics are easier to mold into different shapes than most natural polymers, and they can be tougher, lighter, and more flexible. They also last longer because they are less likely to decay.

The first plastic was made by an English scientist called Alexander Parkes. He called it Parkesine and first showed it to the world in 1851. In 1860 the U.S. scientist John Wesley Hyatt invented a plastic called celluloid, which was later used to make movie film. Both celluloid and Parkesine were used as substitutes for ivory and to make billiard balls. Unfortunately, these early plastics were not stable, and the billiard balls often exploded!

In the early 1900s a race began to find a stable plastic. An English inventor, James Swinburne, was the first to create a stable plastic, but he did not register his discovery immediately. On the day he registered it, he found out that a Belgian-American chemist, Leo Baekeland, had made the same discovery and had registered the plastic the day before.

Baekeland called the plastic Bakelite. It was a hard plastic that could be molded easily into different shapes. Because it did not conduct electricity, it was ideal for making radio cases and electrical equipment. Colored bakelite was used to make objects that had previously been made out of tortoiseshell, saving the lives of thousands of tortoises.

PLASTIC CLOTHES

In 1935 the U.S. scientist Wallace Carothers invented nylon, the first artificial thread. Nylon led the way for the manufacture of other artificial materials, including polyester, dacron, rayon, and kevlar—a tougher version of nylon used for bulletproof vests.

Like many plastics, nylon and polyester are made from chemicals taken from petroleum. These chemicals are converted into polymer molecules and then shaped into small pellets of plastic. To turn the pellets into thread, they are melted, pushed through tiny holes, stretched, and then cooled in water. The thread can then be woven into cloth.

Most artificial polymers are made in factories in vast quantities. In the next activity you will find out how to make your own polymer slime from a few household chemicals.

Polymer structure

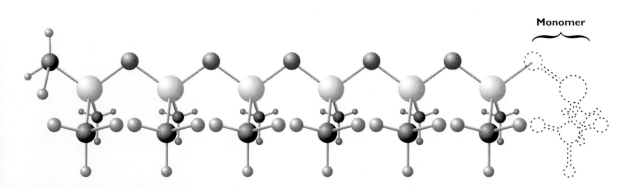

Polymer molecules are long chains made by joining together small molecules, or monomers. (*Mono* is the Greek word for "one," and *poly* is Greek for "many.") The polymer molecules in plastics contain thousands of monomers. For example, a molecule of polyethylene, which is used to make plastic bags, is a chain of about 50,000 molecules of the monomer ethylene.

The polymer above is polydimethylsiloxane. Molecules of this polymer are made up of thousands of molecules of the monomer dimethylsiloxane. Each monomer contains the following elements: carbon (black), oxygen (red), hydrogen (small, dark gray) and silicon (large, light gray).

The silicon in polydimethylsiloxane gives it many useful properties. It repels water and so can be used in waterproofing and to make polishes, like furniture polish. Because silicone does not react with the body's defense systems, polymers like this one can be used to make surgical implants, like false hips and joints.

Slime

Goals

1. **Create a plastic by mixing two materials together.**
2. **Learn more about the properties of polymers.**
3. **Make your own gooey slime.**

What you will need:

- *white glue containing PVA (polyvinyl-acetate)*
- *bowl*
- *food coloring*
- *borax (sodium tetraborate)*
- *¼ cup of water*
- *teaspoon*

Safety tip

Borax is a chemical used in some brands of powdered laundry soap. If you cannot find pure borax in a drugstore, use a laundry soap that contains borax instead. Take care not to touch borax with your bare hands—it might irritate your skin.

1 Pour about ¼ cup of PVA glue into the bowl.

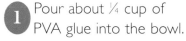

2 Add a few drops of food coloring, and stir well.

3 Add 1 teaspoon of borax to ¼ cup of water, and stir well to make a solution.

4 Pour the borax solution into the bowl, and mix with the glue. The mixture will start to form a gel. It is now safe to touch with your bare hands.

Troubleshooting

What if the slime is too watery and does not form a gel?

If your slime is too watery, try again, but add more borax powder to the water, or add more borax solution to the glue. The more borax you use, the stiffer the slime will get.

5 When the slime has formed a gel, pick it up and squeeze it gently. Some excess water will come out.

Keeping your slime

The slime might get hard over time. If you want to keep it soft, put it in a Ziploc plastic bag in the refrigerator when you are not playing with it.

FOLLOW-UP Slime

You can make several different kinds of slime by simply changing the amounts of borax and glue that you use. The basic recipe is 1 teaspoon of borax powder to ¼ cup of water and the same amount of glue as borax solution.

If you want to experiment with different types of slime, try using 2 tablespoons of borax to one cup of water, instead of 1 teaspoon to ¼ cup of water, and see what happens. Then try using less borax in the solution.

The more borax you use, the thicker your slime will be. If you use enough borax, you can even end up with a hard rubber ball.

The less borax you use, the wetter and stickier the slime will be. Write down your results in a table like the one above so that you can remember how to make the slime you like best.

To make really disgusting, snotty slime, use green food coloring and a small amount of borax. If you add luminous powder as well, your snotty slime will glow in the dark.

Extra bouncy slime
Try the following recipe for a firm slime that will bounce.

Mix 4 teaspoons of water with 5 teaspoons of white PVA glue in a small bowl. Add 1 teaspoon of talcum powder, and stir until mixed. Then add 1 to 2 teaspoons of the borax solution you used in the main activity, and stir for a few minutes. Remove the slime, and knead it for a while. It should get drier.

You might need to dry your hands with a paper towel from time to time, but don't touch the slime with the paper—it will stick. Add talc to the slime to dry it out if it is stickier than you want. When it is dry and rubbery, shape it into a ball, and see if it bounces. If you want to keep it, store it in a Ziploc bag in the refrigerator.

Amount of borax	Amount of water	Amount of glue	Properties of slime
1 teaspoon	¼ cup	¼ cup	slimey
2 tablespoons	1 cup	¼ cup	

ANALYSIS
Artificial materials

You might have guessed from its name that PVA (polyvinylacetate) is a polymer. The long polymer molecules in PVA glue get tangled together, which is what makes the glue thick and sticky. When you add borax (sodium tetraborate) solution, a chemical reaction occurs that changes the polymer molecules. The borax makes the PVA molecules link together, which makes the glue even thicker. Not all of the PVA molecules hook up, though. The more that do, the thicker the slime will get, until it reaches a point where it turns solid. The number of PVA molecules that link together depends partly on the amount of borax in the borax-and-water solution, and partly on how much of the solution you use. Changing the amount of borax or borax solution makes the slime thicker or thinner.

The links that form between the PVA chains in the slime are not strong—they are constantly breaking and re-forming as you play with the slime. When you roll the slime into a ball, the polymer molecules slide over each other and then join up again. If you pull the slime apart suddenly, it breaks as the chains snap.

USING POLYMERS

There are hundreds of different types of plastics. Each type has its own special properties because of the length and shape of its polymer molecules. Polyethylene is the most common plastic, and has a very simple structure. The molecules are long, simple chains that make the plastic tough, flexible, and resistant to chemicals. Plastic bags and drink bottles are made of polyethylene, as well as many other household and industrial objects.

The molecules in nylon (polyamide) make it a very strong plastic even when it is drawn out into a thin thread. Nylon is probably best known for being used to make stockings, but the first nylon item was a toothbrush. Today nylon has all sorts of uses, from rope and clothes to wheels and bearings for motors.

Kevlar is similar to nylon but was invented more recently. It has a very high melting point and is stronger than any other form of nylon. Kevlar is used in heavy-duty conveyor belts, to strengthen tires, and to make bulletproof vests.

Polystyrene is a hard, transparent plastic used to make CD cases and the barrels of ballpoint pens. Sometimes rubber is added to make it tougher. This tough polystyrene is used to make the cases of vacuum cleaners and TVs. A lightweight, bubble-filled form of polystyrene is used in packaging and fast-food containers.

This cyclist's helmet, glasses, and clothes are all made of plastic. His shorts are made of lycra, an artificial fabric that does not lose its shape after being stretched.

The case of this antique radio is made of Bakelite—one of the earliest plastics.

Polyvinylchloride, or PVC, is widely used to make drainpipes, floor tiles, shoes, and raincoats.

Although some plastics can be recycled, most people throw them away when they have finished with them. Since plastics do not decompose (break down) as easily as natural materials, the plastic trash that ends up in the ocean and other places can do great damage to animal and plant life. Plastic can make animals ill if they try to eat it, and many small animals get trapped in plastic packaging or bottles. Always reuse and recycle as much plastic as you can to keep it from causing damage to the environment.

Two different plastics were used to make this toothbrush. The bristles are nylon, and the handle is polyethylene.

ACTIVITY 9
CORROSION

Chemical reactions with air and rain can damage many materials. We call this process corrosion. Some materials take thousands of years to corrode, but others can corrode in an instant.

After years of exposure to air and rain cars eventually corrode. The iron in this car has rusted most where paint has peeled away on the hood.

Have you ever noticed how much shinier a new coin is than an old one, or how cars get rustier with age? Coins and cars gradually change because of the process of corrosion.

Corrosion happens when the atoms on the surface of an object undergo a chemical reaction with atoms from the environment. The chemical reaction produces new substances that change the material's color or texture. These new substances might not bind to the material very tightly, so the material's surface might start to become rough or weak and is more easily worn away by wind or rain. Corrosion is a common problem with many metals. One of the metals that it affects most often is iron.

When iron corrodes, it combines with water and with oxygen molecules from the air to form a new substance called iron oxide, which is reddish-brown in color. It is rust.

Once iron starts to rust, it corrodes at a faster rate. Pure iron is smooth and watertight, but rust is rough and can absorb air and water, which speeds up the rusting process. As rust forms and breaks away from the metal surface, new iron is exposed to air, allowing it to corrode also. Iron structures become weaker when they turn into rust. For this reason it is important that the iron used in cars, machines, or buildings is protected in some way.

SPEED OF CORROSION

There are many different metals, and each one corrodes at a different rate. When the metal potassium touches water, it corrodes so quickly it burns. Rubidium and cesium actually explode when they touch water. If sodium is left in the air, it starts to corrode in just a few minutes.

Other metals corrode slowly. Platinum and gold are very special because the pure metals do not corrode at all in air. This is why platinum is used to make electrodes and electronic circuits, and why gold is so popular in jewelry.

There are lots of ways to prevent corrosion. One of the easiest is to paint metals or coat them with plastic. This outer layer acts as a barrier between the metal and the air; but if cracks form, the metal will corrode quickly.

Another method is to coat the metal with a different metal that corrodes more slowly. Galvanized iron is protected this way. A layer of zinc on its surface corrodes slower than the iron and so prevents rusting. The iron stays undamaged even if the zinc gets scratched. Garbage cans, iron pipes, and corrugated metal roofs are made from galvanized iron.

A very good way to prevent corrosion is to combine different metals by mixing them when they are molten. The resulting mixture is called an alloy. Stainless steel, for instance, is an alloy of iron, chromium, and nickel that is completely rustproof.

Precious objects, like metal statues, are sometimes covered with gold to stop corrosion. This also looks very nice, but it is expensive.

Patina and tarnish

A thin layer of corrosion on metals is sometimes called a patina or tarnish. Patinas can have many colors and can be very beautiful. Many artists and sculptors deliberately use metals that will corrode to leave a pretty patina.

Bronze is a metal that quickly acquires a lovely green patina and is often used to make statues and pots. Copper also reacts quickly with oxygen to form a blue-green patina that can be cleaned off with a mild acid such as lemon juice. Silver reacts with oxygen to form a black patina. If your parents have silver cutlery or dishes in the cupboard, they probably have to clean them sometimes with silver polish to remove the patina and make them shiny.

The next time you are in a museum, take a look at some old metal pots and statues, and see if you can tell what metal they were made from by the color of the patina.

This bronze pot was made between 1766 B.C. and 1045 B.C. It was used for storing wine.

ACTIVITY

Studying Rust

Goals

1. **Learn why materials rust.**
2. **Find out what substances cause or prevent rusting.**
3. **Study the rate of rusting.**

What you will need:

- 6 iron nails
- 6 small jars with lids
- tap water
- boiled water
- vegetable oil
- 2 tablespoons of salt
- spoon

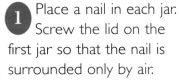

1 Place a nail in each jar. Screw the lid on the first jar so that the nail is surrounded only by air.

2 Pour in enough water to cover the nail in the second jar with tap water, and screw the lid on.

3 In the third jar pour in enough boiled water to cover the nail. Then pour in 2 tablespoons of oil to make a film of oil on the surface. Screw the lid on the jar.

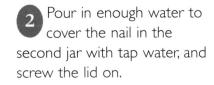

4 In the fourth jar half-cover the nail with tap water so that the top half of the nail is in the air. Then screw on the lid.

5 In the fifth jar pour in enough tap water to completely cover the nail. Then add 2 tablespoons of salt, and screw on the lid.

Which is which?

Make sure that you label each jar so that you know which is which. When measuring the rust, always return the jars to the same place.

6 Fill the sixth jar almost to the top with tap water, dip the nail in some oil, place the oily nail into the jar, and screw on the lid.

7 Check the jars for signs of rust at regular intervals over the next week.

FOLLOW-UP Studying rust

The rust might form very quickly, so you should check the jars frequently on the first day. Don't take the rusty nails out of the jars—that would spoil the experiment. Instead, use the jar like a lens to look at how much rust has formed on each nail. Write down your results, and keep a note of the time so that you can record how quickly the rust forms.

If you have sharp eyesight, you could try to estimate what percentage of each nail is rusty each time you check them.

You could repeat the experiment with other liquids. Cover one nail with lemon juice, another with vinegar, and a third with water. Which rusts fastest?

You can also use other metals to see if they corrode faster or slower than iron. Copper is a good metal to try because it also corrodes quickly.

When you've found out which jar makes nails rust most quickly, experiment with different ways of

You can make a 3-D display of your results, but after a few days all the nails will be covered with rust.

protecting the nails. Coat several nails with different materials, such as wax, paint, tape, or tinfoil. Then place each one in a jar with ideal conditions for fast rusting.

The "tin" cans that tinned food comes in are really made from steel coated with a thin layer of tin to keep the steel from rusting. Carry out the following experiment to find out how effective this tin layer is.

Take two empty tin cans, and soak them in water to remove the labels. Make sure the cans have no sharp edges. Flatten one, and try to damage its surface by rubbing it with sandpaper or a brillo pad, or by scratching it with a nail. Place both cans in solutions of warm salt water, and leave them for a few days. On which can does rust appear first?

ANALYSIS
Corrosion

The corrosion of iron is caused by a complex chemical reaction. Oxygen and water must both be present. Other chemicals, such as salt and acid, can speed up the process.

The nail you put in air alone probably did not rust, because there was no water in the jar. In contrast, the nail you put in salty water rusted very quickly because it had both oxygen and water, as well as salt to speed up the reaction. What about the other nails?

Oxygen is not just in the air—it also dissolves in water. Tap water contains dissolved oxygen, so an iron object submerged in tap water will rust even though it is not in contact with the air. However, when water boils, the oxygen comes out in the form of bubbles. The nail in the boiled water did not rust quickly because there was less oxygen in its water. The film of oil on the water kept oxygen in the air from entering the water.

The nail you dipped in oil had a protective layer that helped slow down rusting, but the protection was not perfect. Some of the oil came off and allowed water to touch the nail.

If you repeated the experiment with lemon juice and vinegar, you would have found that the nails rusted much more quickly. Lemon juice and vinegar are weak acids, and acids speed up the process of corrosion.

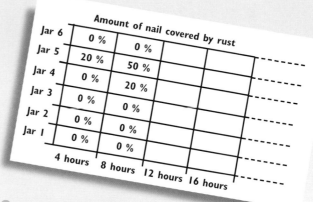

	Amount of nail covered by rust			
Jar 6	0 %	0 %		
Jar 5	20 %	50 %		
Jar 4	0 %	20 %		
Jar 3	0 %	0 %		
Jar 2	0 %	0 %		
Jar 1	0 %	0 %		
	4 hours	8 hours	12 hours	16 hours

You can record how quickly rust forms on the different nails by making a table like this one.

STOPPING CORROSION

One of the new ways of protecting against corrosion is through the use of artificial materials that can respond to stress and other physical changes. Many buildings are made of concrete with iron or steel reinforcements running through the center. As the concrete ages, it cracks, which lets air and moisture reach the iron. If the iron rusts, the building may weaken, and whole sections might need to be replaced. In some modern buildings the concrete contains plastic fibers filled with a chemical, called an anticorrosive agent, that stops corrosion. When cracks form in the concrete, the outer coating of the plastic fibers starts to dissolve. This releases the anticorrosive agent, which then keeps the iron or steel from rusting.

Metal corrosion is the most common form of corrosion, but corrosion can affect other materials, too. Stone buildings and statues are sometimes corroded by acid rain. This is a very damaging type of pollution that can kill trees and poison lakes, as well as corrode buildings. Acid rain is caused by a chemical called sulfur dioxide, which comes from car exhausts and power plants. Sulfur dioxide in the air combines with rain to produce a weak acid. This acid reacts with the stone in buildings and statues, weakening the surface. Over time the surface crumbles away. Acid rain is slowly ruining the Taj Mahal in India, the Parthenon in Greece, and many other priceless buildings around the world.

Corrosion caused by acid rain has damaged this stonework on Durham Cathedral in England.

ACTIVITY 10

RECYCLING

When we have finished using a material, we usually just throw it out. But many materials can be reused, or recycled, to make more materials. This saves a lot of energy and resources, and does less harm to the environment.

In nature nothing is wasted. Organisms called decomposers eat dead material and give off nutrients in their waste. These nutrients are then used as the raw materials for new plants and animals to live and grow. All the natural materials in the environment are recycled in this way.

Humans are not quite so efficient. Many of the artificial materials we use, such as plastics, do not decay when we throw them away. Instead, they build up in vast garbage dumps that can damage the environment. To make matters worse, a lot of these materials are made from "nonrenewable resources," which means there is only a limited supply on our planet. Plastics, for example, come from fossil fuels, such as petroleum, coal, and natural gas. Our supplies of fossil fuels could run out in 50–100 years, so we might have to stop making plastics.

One way around this problem is to figure out ways of recycling the materials we use. This not only makes them last longer but also reduces the amount of garbage we produce, so recycling helps prevent damage to the environment.

Lots of materials can be recycled, including metals, glass, plastics, and paper. To make recycling easier, people throw different types of garbage into different bins. The materials are then collected and purified before recycling can begin.

Glass is recycled by crushing it into small pieces, melting them in a furnace, and then pouring out the glass into molds to make new bottles or other objects. Metals are crushed, shredded, and then they, too, are melted and poured out for reuse.

Recycling bins make it easier for people to sort used cans, bottles, and paper for recycling.

One of the most important metals that we recycle is aluminum, which is used in soft drink cans, foil containers, and other products. New aluminum is very expensive to produce because extracting the metal from rock is a complicated process.

Plastics are difficult to recycle because there are many different kinds, and each has to be recycled separately. Even a ketchup bottle contains six different kinds of plastic. As a result, a lot of plastic still ends up in garbage dumps. Scientists have invented plastics that decay—biodegradable plastics—but they are not yet in common use.

TREES AND PAPER

Although wood is a natural material, it is also a limited resource. There are two main types of wood: hardwood and softwood. Hardwood comes from trees like maple and walnut, and is used for high-quality furniture. A hardwood forest takes hundreds of years to grow and supports many different species, but the wood is in such demand that hardwood forests are shrinking all over the world.

Softwood trees, such as pine, are used for making paper and timber for buildings. To save trees and forests, it is important to recycle paper. To do this, waste paper is shredded, washed, and bleached

Crates of aluminum cans await processing at a recycling center in Tokyo Bay, Japan. In some countries up to two-thirds of aluminum cans are recycled.

to remove ink and dirt. Then the paper is mixed with water and ground to a pulp. The pulp is then rolled flat and dried. Recycled paper can be used for many of the same jobs as new paper. In Japan half the paper that people use has been recycled. This saves millions of trees each year.

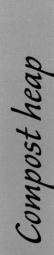

Compost heap

Compost heaps produce heat in the center. Keep the heat in by covering the heap with a piece of old carpet or sacking.

The wooden frame around this compost heap allows air to enter the compost.

The compost heap contains layers of kitchen scraps and dead plants with layers of dirt between.

After several months nutritious compost will form. Use it to fertilize plants in your garden.

You can recycle natural materials yourself. Instead of throwing away kitchen scraps, lawn cuttings, and dead plants, make a compost heap. You can use compost to give the plants in your garden extra nutrients. Place dead leaves, potato peelings, and uneaten fruit or vegetables in layers inside a large container outside. Make sure the container is open to the air. Cover each layer with some soil, and keep the pile moist. Microorganisms will eat the rotting material and gradually turn it into compost over several months.

Recycled Paper

Goals

1. **Learn how to recycle paper.**
2. **Find out how recycling affects the properties of a material.**

What you will need:

- *waste paper*
- *large glass of water*
- *mixing bowl*
- *tray*

Colored paper

Add water-based paint or food coloring to the pulp to give the paper color. Or, try using magazines for a more interesting recycled paper.

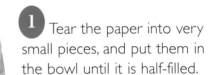

1 Tear the paper into very small pieces, and put them in the bowl until it is half-filled.

2 Pour in enough water to cover the paper, and leave it to soak for about 15 minutes.

3 Squeeze and mash the paper well with your hands until it has broken down to make a big gloppy mess—paper pulp.

4 Squeeze excess water out of the pulp with your hands.

5 Press the pulp onto the tray, and spread it out thinly and evenly.

Messy business

Making paper is messy, so make sure you do it somewhere that will be easy to clean up. To make smoother paper, ask an adult to grind up the pulp in a blender. Make sure you wash the blender thoroughly afterward. Leave the paper to dry on a flat surface rather than hanging it up, since the wet paper will not be strong enough to hang.

Troubleshooting

What if the paper is too thick and stiff to use for projects?

To make your paper thinner, lay some screen or mesh over the tray, and flatten the pulp with a rolling pin.

Some types of paper might need to soak for a long time before the paper breaks down. Make sure you mash the pulp well with your hands, or ask an adult to use a blender.

6 Leave the paper to dry in a warm place. If you want to dry it quickly, ask an adult to place it in the oven at about 100°F (38°C) for a few hours, with the door open a crack.

7 When the paper is dry, gently peel it away from the tray.

FOLLOW-UP Recycled paper

Paper was originally made by mixing rags with wood to make a very tough form of paper. You can make rag paper by shredding some old cotton and adding the shreds to torn-up paper. Then add water to make pulp, as in the main activity.

Some paper is made from sawdust. Add sawdust to the paper mix, and see if it makes better paper.

Try rolling your paper pulp into sheets of different thicknesses. Then compare the sheets to see which is strongest, and which absorbs the most water. Compare these properties to the original paper that you recycled. In what ways are they different?

You could also try molding paper pulp in a bowl or a cup, instead of pressing it flat.

ANALYSIS
Recycling

The word paper comes from papyrus, the Latin name for an ancient writing material made from the reeds of an Egyptian plant. The Egyptians made papyrus by pounding the reeds and then laying them in the sun to dry and form a sheet. According to Chinese legend, the first person to make paper from pulp was a man called Cai Lun, who presented a sheet of paper to the Chinese emperor in 105 A.D. It was made from fishing nets, rags, and tree bark.

All paper is made from fibers—long strands of material. Most modern paper is made from wood fiber. Some of this wood fiber comes from sawdust and other waste materials produced by sawmills in timber plants.

The length of the fibers in paper affect its properties. Wood pulp has long fibers that clump together to form strong, smooth paper that does not absorb water quickly. In recycled paper the fibers are shorter because they get torn up when they are made into pulp again. As a result, recycled paper is weaker than new paper. It also has a rougher surface, which makes it absorb water more easily and become soggy. In paper-recycling plants fresh sawdust is often added to give the paper more strength.

YOUR PAPER

When you soaked your waste paper in water, the wood fibers in the paper loosened. They then separated and tore apart as you mashed the paper up or blended it into pulp. The more you mash and squish the pulp, the more the fibers separate. This makes the pulp more flexible and produces better paper.

The fibers rearranged when you pressed the pulp into the tray, and they stuck together as the paper dried. It is important to dry the paper well—it gets stronger as it gets drier.

Because you did not remove the color from your paper, it will not be very useful for writing on. However, you can paint on it or use it as a background paper for art projects. In commercial recycling the pulp is bleached to remove all the color and make it white before it is rolled into paper sheets.

REDUCE, REUSE, RECYCLE

Take a few minutes to think about how many materials you and your family throw away every day. Everything you throw away might contain valuable materials that could be used again, instead of being left in a dump and harming the environment. You can help save the planet from becoming dirty and ugly by following the three rules for keeping the planet green. Reduce, Reuse, and Recycle.

The first step is to reduce the amount of materials that you use. Then reuse materials if you can. Finally, recycle everything that can be recycled.

Now that you know how to recycle paper, you can help protect the environment. Save waste paper instead of throwing it away, and recycle it into wrapping paper, birthday cards, or paintings.

Recycling the trash

Plastics are sorted into different types before recycling. Then they are cleaned and shredded into chips that can be melted down and molded into new products.

Aluminum cans are heated to remove labels and paint, then melted and poured into molds to make new cans and other products.

Old wood can be ground up and turned into sawdust to be used for making paper or pressboard, which is used in construction.

Glass bottles are separated by color and cleaned. The glass is ground up, melted, and then made into new bottles.

Newspaper, magazines, cardboard, and waste papers are pulped to separate the fibers, then recycled into new paper.

Leftover food and dead plants can be recycled by placing them on a compost heap. Tiny organisms called decomposers eat the rotting remains and convert them into a nutritious compost for plants.

GLOSSARY

adhesive: A wet substance that is spread over surfaces and then left to dry to hold the objects together. Another word for glue.

afterbath: A rinse given to a fabric after it has been dyed to change its color.

alloy: A mixture of two or more metals, or a metal mixed with a nonmetal such as carbon.

atom: The basic unit of an element. In an element all atoms share the same number of subatomic particles called protons and electrons.

boiling point: The temperature at which a liquid becomes a gas.

bond: The chemical link between two or more atoms. Bonds are created during chemical reactions between substances.

chemical structure: The three-dimensional arrangement of atoms in a molecule, which affects the properties of the substance.

chemical reaction: The process by which atoms or compounds bond or split to make new substances.

compost: Vegetable matter that is left to rot (with the help of decomposers) and that provides a nutritious food for plants.

compound: A substance made of atoms of more than one element. The smallest unit of a compound is called a molecule.

crystal: A substance that has a definite and regular shape. Ice, for example, forms six-sided crystals that create the shapes of snowflakes.

decomposer: Organisms, such as fungi and bacteria, that break down dead organisms and feces.

dissolve: When the atoms of a liquid, a solid, or a gas (called solutes) separate and combine so thoroughly with the atoms of a liquid or gas (the solvent) that a solution is made.

drug: A chemical made in a laboratory or extracted from a plant or animal that is used as a medicine to treat diseases in people (and sometimes animals).

dye: A substance, often a solution, that is used to color fabrics or other materials.

element: A substance that is made of only one kind of atom. Oxygen is an element, but water is a compound—a combination of atoms of the two elements oxygen and hydrogen.

evaporate: To change from a liquid into a gas.

fixer: A chemical added to a dye bath that helps the fabric being dyed hold onto the color. Fixers include salt and alum, and they are also called mordants.

fossil fuel: A substance, such as coal or natural gas, that was formed from decayed plants or animals over millions of years and is is burned to produce energy.

freezing point: The temperature at which a liquid becomes a solid.

galvanized: Metal covered with a layer of zinc.

impurity: Unwanted substance mixed in with a useful substance. In salt extraction any mud particles mixed in with the salt would be called impurities.

laser: A powerful beam of light of one color that travels in a straight line. Lasers are used in printing, science, surgery, and communication.

magnetic: A substance that can attract iron and has a magnetic field. Iron is the most common magnetic substance.

melting point: The temperature at which a solid becomes a liquid.

mineral: Solid compounds found in rocks. Rocks are usually made up of several different minerals. Each type of mineral has the same chemical composition and the same properties. Quartz, for example, is made of silicon dioxide and forms six-sided crystals.

molecule: A group of atoms that are linked (bonded) together. Molecules are the smallest parts of compounds.

natural gas: A mixture of gases formed millions of years ago from decaying organisms. It is mined from under the ground and is an important fossil fuel.

nutrient: Any substance that a living organism uses as food, such as starch in a potato or nitrates taken from soil by a plant's roots.

ore: Metal mixed with rock that is mined from the ground and treated to produce a pure metal. Hematite, an iron ore, is heated with other substances to give up its iron.

paint: A colored liquid that is spread over an object and left to dry to give it color.

petroleum: The black oil that is mined from deep under the ground, where it formed millions of years ago from living organisms. Petroleum is made into a range of products from gasoline to plastics.

pigment: A substance that gives color. Pigments range from the chlorophyll that makes plants green to the compounds that color glass.

plastic: One of several hundred types of material, several of which are made from petroleum.

polymer: Giant molecule made of one type of molecule (a monomer) repeated many times. Hair, wool, and plastic bags are polymers.

properties: The features of a substance or a material such as hardness, color, or smell.

protein: A substance made by organisms for a huge range of jobs, including driving cell reactions or building body parts such as muscles. Protein is eaten in foods like meat and fish.

residue: The part left behind (often a solid) after a liquid has evaporated or been filtered.

smelting: The heat-driven process by which iron is extracted from its ore.

solute: A liquid, a solid, or a gas that mixes so thoroughly into a liquid that it makes a solution.

solution: A mixture of a liquid (the solvent) with a liquid, solid, or gas (the solute). The atoms of the solute scatter evenly among the atoms of the solvent.

solvent: A liquid or gas that can dissolve a liquid, gas, or solid.

starch: A food substance (consisting of many glucose molecules) made and stored by plants.

vapor: A substance in its gaseous state. Often used to describe water when it is a gas—water vapor.

x-ray: A kind of radiation that is similar to light but invisible to human eyes. X-rays travel through some substances more easily than others and are used to create pictures of bones or crystals.

SET INDEX